This is an awesome book, and every parent ought to read it with their children and talk about the awesome fact that *Bumps are Okay*!

DR. STEVE HARNEY
FOUNDER OF COOL KIDS MINISTRIES

Packed with information on monster trucks, *Bumps are Okay* is a captivating set of lessons for your class. Sharon Czerwien springboards into Biblical application on subjects like surviving hard times, obeying the rules, and finding the proper help. Perfect for what kids need today.

GAIL GRITTS
BLOGGER AND TEACHER
AUTHOR OF *THE REBA AND KATHERINE SERIES*
AND *THERE'S A HOLE IN MY SOCK*

BUMPS ARE OKAY FOR KIDS
and Other Biblical Lessons Learned from Monster Trucks!

Published by Lucid Books in Houston, TX
www.LucidBooks.com

ISBN: 978-1-63296-557-8
eISBN: 978-1-63296-558-5

Special Sales: Lucid Books titles are available in special quantity discounts. Custom imprinting or excerpting can also be done to fit special needs. Contact Lucid Books at Info@LucidBooks.com

LUCIDBOOKS

BUMPS ARE OKAY

FOR KIDS

and Other Biblical Lessons
Learned from Monster Trucks!

SHARON CZERWIEN

Driving Point #1

MONSTER TRUCK DRIVERS MUST AGREE THAT BUMPS ARE OKAY!

God has a purpose for your bumps!

Driving Point #2

MONSTER TRUCKS NEED A GOOD SUSPENSION SYSTEM TO
PROPERLY BOUNCE AND OPERATE ON THEIR BUMPY RIDES.

A spiritual suspension system is necessary to
survive your life's bumps!

Driving Point #3

MONSTER TRUCKS HAVE A STURDY AND STRONG
FRAME TO SURVIVE THE BUMPS.

The Bible is the important spiritual frame to
handle your bumps!

Driving Point #4

MONSTER TRUCKS DO NOT HAVE FULLY AIRED-UP TIRES.

There are shocking "WOAH moments" in life—just like with
the deflated-looking monster truck tires.

Driving Point #5

MONSTER TRUCK DRIVERS MUST PERSEVERE.

There is a need to persevere in the middle of life's bumps.

Driving Point #6

MONSTER TRUCKS CAN BE JOLTING AND DIZZYING.

Life can be jolting and dizzying at times!
Remember Who is always with you.

Driving Point #7
MONSTER TRUCK DRIVERS MUST SUBMIT TO THE TRACK OFFICIALS.
There are important "track officials" who have
authority in your life.

Driving Point #8
MONSTER TRUCK DRIVERS NEED HELP FROM OTHER EXPERTS.
God has placed needed "experts" in your life.

Driving Point #9
MONSTER TRUCK DRIVERS MUST BE PREPARED.
Spiritual preparation and armor are both necessary
to deal with spiritual temptations.

Driving Point #10
MONSTER TRUCKS ARE BUILT FROM LIGHTWEIGHT PARTS.
When you feel weighed down with stress,
cast your worries to God!

Driving Point #11
MONSTER TRUCK SEATS ARE FIT SPECIFICALLY TO THE DRIVER.
Remember to make the Bible be at home in your heart.

Driving Point #12
MONSTER TRUCKS SOMETIMES GET DIRTY AND MESSED UP!
Even when you get spiritually dirty and messed up,
God can forgive you and use you again!

Introduction

Hello there! I am very excited that you want to learn more about monster trucks. My son LOVES all things monster trucks. Thanks to him, I have learned much about them along the way, too.

The more I learn about monster trucks, the more excited I get about some of the biblical lessons we can learn from them.

**LEARNING BIBLE LESSONS
FROM MONSTER TRUCKS SEEMS CRAZY,
I KNOW!**

In this book, you will read about twelve interesting characteristics of monster trucks and their drivers. You will then learn specific biblical lessons that match up with these characteristics.

Hang on and hold tight. You will have the chance to see that *bumps* are okay. Plus, I invite you to check out the other biblical lessons you can learn from monster trucks.

Sharon

About the Book

Each of the twelve sections of the book has three main parts:

1. THE DRIVING POINT

Each *Driving Point* gives an interesting characteristic about monster trucks or the drivers. There are twelve *Driving Points* in all.

For this book, I share what I learned in my interviews with award-winning Monster Jam ® driver, Brianna Mahon (driver of WHIPLASH), and a Monster Jam ® Crew Chief. Brianna and this Crew Chief share interesting monster truck facts.

2. THE BIBLE TAKEAWAY

Each *Bible Takeaway* gives the biblical lesson that matches up with each *Driving Point*.

3. THE APPLICATION

In each *Application* section, I share specific examples of how you can apply the biblical lessons learned from monster trucks.

> » At the end of the book, you will find many great books and websites to learn more about monster trucks and their drivers.

I learned interesting information about monster trucks, drivers, and the *Bible Takeaways* from the books and websites listed on the back of this book. In this same section, you will also see all the names of the interesting people whom I interviewed.

#1

Driving Point #1

Do you enjoy hayrides? Have you ever been on one that drove through mud and intense bumps? On the other hand, have you ever tried taking a nap on a road trip while your parent drove down a very bumpy road?

Are some bumps more fun than others?
Do some bumps completely irritate you?

Some people who seem to really enjoy bumps are monster truck drivers. They must accept that they will experience intense bumps during their rallies. If the drivers cannot handle these bumps, then they are probably in the wrong field of work!

These drivers experience hard landings and are at risk of crashing into other monster trucks during their races. These brave drivers willingly bump into walls and obstacles. They drive over cars!

According to MonsterJam.com, driver Cynthia Gauthier drove her monster truck directly upwards on her high jump with a height of over 45 feet! This jump took place during the Monster Jam World Finals XX. Imagine the bumpy landing after that high jump.

Though Cynthia landed hard, she was still able to make a great save. Right after, she stuck her head out her truck's window and excitedly banged on the top of her truck.

I have a feeling that some of the bumps are exciting for the drivers. Yet, some are probably unpleasant (and unplanned). Either way, the drivers know that bumps come with the job. They must accept the good and the bad bumps in order to compete.

Bible Takeaway:

Life can sure be *bumpy*, too! What do I mean by this?

Life can be filled with hardships and difficulties. The Bible sometimes calls these **bumps** "trials." Here is an example from the book of James in the New Testament:

> Consider it all joy, my brothers and sisters, when you encounter various trials, knowing that the testing of your faith produces endurance. (James 1:2-3)

This does not mean that God expects you to say, "Yay, yay, yay, I am going through a hard trial! I am thrilled to be experiencing a life *bump*!"

Verse two listed above just means that you can keep your joy, even in the hard times.

God does not expect you to be joyful <u>for</u> your *bumps*. With God's strength, you can be joyful <u>during</u> the *bumps*.

This sounds crazy, I know! It is mind-blowing.
How is this even possible?

It comes down to seeing the big picture. Monster truck drivers must sometimes go through a bumpy path to reach the end of their exciting run. Sometimes you must go through a difficulty to reach a goal.

What is the goal, though? Is it even worth it?

The goal is spiritual growth. Specifically, when you keep your joy <u>during</u> a life's *bump*, you are growing in your spiritual **endurance** (James 1:3). You are growing your "spiritual muscles." As a result, you can learn to trust God more and more through life's difficulties.

Just as monster truck drivers are athletes, so are runners. I interviewed an **endurance** runner. His name is Brad Williams. He has completed eleven marathons, including the Boston Marathon two different times.

Mr. Williams spoke about the intensity that his body had to go through so that he could compete well. In his early training days, his muscles would feel strained. His body would be completely exhausted and worn. He told me that his body would feel "total misery."

He remembered his specific goals, though. He wanted to qualify for the Boston Marathon and compete in Ironman Triathlons.

Mr. Williams mentioned there was a good purpose for straining his body. He knew in the long run that the muscle pain would allow his muscles to strengthen. Pushing hard brought soreness, but he knew that once the muscles were repaired, they would be stronger!

How could an athlete possibly find purpose in pain?

Any athlete must first go through much pain. Spiritually speaking, you will sometimes be spiritually stretched in a trial. God can use any trial to grow your endurance, though. These *bumps* can stretch you and grow your spiritual muscles.

This is how you can keep your joy <u>during</u> life's *bumps*. You know God is up to something good. He wants to help you increase your faith and trust Him more in any trial.

Application:

I do not know any details about the current *bumps* you are experiencing.

Is school difficult for you? Did your parents recently tell you that your family cannot afford for you to play in the expensive soccer league? Has your best friend recently moved away? Did you just find out that you have food sensitivities and cannot eat the same foods as your friends? Is your favorite uncle in the military and living overseas? Do you worry about your grandma's illness? Do any classmates make fun of you in school? Do you worry about other things?

I feel your pain. I have children who experience difficulties in life. I wish I could keep them from their pain. However, all of us must remember that *bumps are okay*. God has designed life in such a way that we spiritually grow *in* our *bumps*. We learn to endure trials and grow stronger from them.

It may take a while to believe it, but I encourage you to try and think about these words...*bumps are okay.*

Bumps are okay!

They truly do have a good purpose.

Application Questions:

» What is one current *bump* that is causing you much stress?

» In the past, what was the most difficult *bump* that you had to *endure*? (What difficulty did you have to go through, yet you survived?)

» How did you handle that past difficulty? (Did you complain? Did you get angry or stay calm? Did you ask for help? Did you pray about it?)

» Have you ever considered that a trial can cause you to become spiritually stronger?

#2

Driving Point #2

When you were younger, did you ever play "too roughly" with one of your toy monster trucks (or any toy in general)? Did your mom or grandma *cringe* when you bounced your monster truck "too much?" (I have been guilty of cringing!) All along, you knew how much your truck could handle, though, right?

You just read how monster truck drivers must accept their bumps. Thankfully, the monster trucks truly can handle their bumpy rides quite well! They are well-designed to handle their huge, bumpy landings. This is all thanks to a well-made suspension system.

The *Monster Jam Official Guidebook* teaches that a good suspension system is what allows monster trucks to survive the impact of big landings. As you may have seen, real monster trucks bounce hard!

Two main parts of the suspension system are the shock absorbers and springs. The shock absorbers and springs absorb the movements of the monster trucks. Specifically, the springs squeeze to then soak up any bumps before bouncing back to the typical length.

Did you know that MonsterJam.com has a lot of great information under the "Education and Activities" heading? Under the "Monster Shocks" category, you can learn that each monster truck has eight shocks. Shocks are extremely necessary for the drivers to operate their stunts well. This same part of the website teaches that shocks are one of the most important parts of the monster trucks.

In the book, *Monster Trucks*, the author teaches that strong shocks are needed to help monster trucks land the distance of 100-foot jumps! (That is the length of ten basketball goals laid side by side.)

It would be a waste of time to watch monster truck rallies if the trucks could never survive *any* landings after getting "Big Air" or if they could not withstand the landings on any "Slap Wheelies!"

Bible Takeaway:

A SPIRITUAL SUSPENSION SYSTEM IS NECESSARY TO SURVIVE YOUR LIFE'S *BUMPS*!

If monster trucks require a good suspension system for physical bumps, you and your friends need a good spiritual *suspension system* for the unexpected *bumps* in life.

Remember that monster trucks are designed to survive big bumps. How has God designed for you to survive life's *bumps*?

The Bible describes the importance of relying on God as your refuge and strength. Here is what one of the Psalms teaches:

> **God is our refuge and strength, a very ready help in trouble. Therefore we will not fear, though the earth shakes and the mountains slip into the heart of the sea. (Psalm 46:1-2)**

There are two keywords in verse one above:

REFUGE

This word has to do with a place of safety or protection. Think of the audience at an outdoor monster truck rally. If it started to downpour, many people would probably rush to be under some kind of covering. This covering would be considered their *refuge*.

God is your refuge. He is your safety when you are in a life difficulty. You can run to Him in prayer and trust that He will be your covering and safety in your tough situation.

STRENGTH

God is also your strength. You do not have to use your own strength to get through a trial. You can rest in the strength of God to help you through your hard times. The end of verse one teaches that God is *very ready* to help you.

Verse two is there to encourage you with the following. Because God is offering you HIS available help to bring you through your hard times, you can give your fears to Him. In your scary times, God is at work in your life and is ready to offer you *strength*.

Application:

Since *bumps are okay*, how can you survive them? You can survive them by trusting God to give you a place of safety and His strength during your specific trials. God's available and promised *refuge* and *strength* are like your promised spiritual suspension system!

This is a difficult concept for adults to accept. Is it really that simple? Can God truly give you the strength to survive your hard *bumps* just by trusting in His offer to provide you necessary strength?

It is truly a matter of faith. Praise God, YES, He does follow through on His end to help you through your trials. You can take your stresses and fears to God. You can pray to God for His help to make it through. You can allow God to be like your suspension system.

During a recording of a Monster Jam rally in Anaheim, California, there was an interesting conversation between a few of the broadcasters. Bari Musawwir emphasized that a driver must make sure his shocks are working at 100%. Bari then said, "You want to be able to put your truck through its paces, and in order to do that, you have to make sure your shocks are in tip-top shape."

Unfortunately, you will certainly be put through your paces in life (just like a monster truck that Bari spoke about). Life will turn *bumpy* at times. Trials will strike and bounce you in more ways than you may desire. You can rest in the fact that God is there to strengthen you while you go through your hardships. Let God be your suspension system for your spiritual *bumps*.

A specific prayer example (based on the words of Psalm 46) may look like the following in your specific situations:

School:

God, school is hard right now. I am overwhelmed in my classes. Thank you that I can turn to you for strength to get me through each school hour. Please help me to survive sitting in my classes, and help me know who to ask for help with my schoolwork. Until that point, help me not to fear, even though I feel that my grades are sinking and school is bringing me down. Help me to trust You to help me through this trial.

Amen

Friends

God, things are quite awkward with friends right now. We are going through things, and I do not know who is mad at me or what has gone wrong. Please help me to find my help and strength in You. Thank you that You are always ready to help. Even though it feels like my friends are slipping away and things are always awkward, help me not to fear my situation. Please give me wisdom on how to handle this and from what adult to seek assistance.

Amen

It is important to truly place your hope in the promises of Psalm 46:1-2. God is ready to answer your cry for help. Please be encouraged that you can drive through your *bumps* trusting God and His good purposes.

Application Questions:

» How is your "spiritual suspension system" when your life feels too "bouncy" for your liking? (Are you bringing your fears and concerns to God in prayer?)

» What are some examples of things that provide you protection during severe weather? (Umbrella, rainboots?)

» How can you ask God to protect you during a difficulty?

» You can use the above example prayers if you need help on how to pray during difficult times.

#3

Driving Point #3

Have you ever studied about your skeleton? Have you ever thought about the importance of the structure and stability that your skeleton provides? Your skeleton is like your frame.

On the same note, have you ever thought about your vehicle's frame? This frame is like the "backbone" of your vehicle.

Monster trucks have a protective frame. This frame can also be called a roll cage or chassis. The *Monster Jam Official Guidebook* calls this frame a **skeleton**. This skeleton is made of strong material, which helps protect the trucks and drivers in the best and safest possible way.

I was able to interview a Monster Jam ® Crew Chief. He said the frame can be made from Chromoly tubing or mild steel. The Crew Chief said that both make good choices for the frame. Choosing between the two depends on the person building the frame. The point is, that either choice makes for a sturdy and strong frame.

A strong frame is necessary. It is not just a recommendation. The drivers NEED this strong frame. First, it provides support to the important parts of the truck (the body and especially the engine). The last thing monster truck drivers want is for their trucks to completely crumble on impact.

Secondly, but most importantly, the strong frame keeps drivers safe from otherwise pending destruction. It is important that monster truck drivers have protection while inside the cab of the truck. A sturdy and strong frame is that important!

Bible Takeaway:

A strong frame is crucial for the well-being of any driver. The same is true for anyone's spiritual well-being.

In this same way, any building must have a strong frame (and foundation). Without a strong frame and foundation, simple *bumps* will ruin the building.

Jesus spoke specifically about the importance of a spiritual frame and foundation. When trials happen, those without a solid frame will experience much stress.

What is this spiritual frame, though?
The spiritual frame involves paying attention
to what the Bible teaches.

In Matthew 7:24-27, Jesus spoke about the difference between people who pay attention to God's Word (the Bible) and those who ignore it.

The person who pays attention to the Bible is compared to a house with a strong and sturdy *foundation* on a rock. When hard times happen, this person is not destroyed. He or she can trust in God's plan and survive the trial.

The person who ignores the Bible in life is likened to a house that is built on a weak foundation (the sand). When hard times strike, this person will not do well without God's strength.

I like how the Bible talks about the Bible being like a "rock." The Bible is a solid and sturdy help in hard times. The Bible also mentions that God is our rock.

In Psalm and 2 Samuel, there are very similar verses about God being like a "rock."

For who is God, but the LORD? And who is a rock, except our God, the God who encircles me with strength... (Psalm 18:31-32a)

For who is God, except the LORD?
And who is a rock, except our God?
God is my strong fortress... (2 Samuel 22:32-33a)

Spiritual strength can be small at times. Life's *bumps* can frustrate and weaken anyone. The only way to have the spiritual strength to make it through a hard situation is to trust God and His promise. He is like a sturdy, spiritual frame.

Application:

Put together, what does all this mean? Sure, you understand that a strong frame is protective on a truck. How is God a strong and sturdy frame in your life?

Life is filled with obstacles and random events to overcome (much like in each monster truck rally). Examples of life obstacles are:

- Not being accepted in the new robotics club

- Not earning a spot on the basketball team

- Getting sick and missing a lot of school/feeling behind in your school subjects

- Not getting the prized spot in your school's music program

- Having a new food allergy that keeps you from enjoying all the same foods that your friends can

- Not being able to walk, see, or hear as well as your classmates

- Not having the money to own all the nice clothes that your classmates do

- Having a broken arm and missing out on all the fun after school or on the weekends

There are so many possibilities!

Monster truck drivers can look at their track obstacles in one of two ways. The obstacles are just something new to overcome. On the other hand, they can be seen as something that makes the drivers scared, mad, or frustrated, and the drivers just give up.

In the middle of your life's obstacles, you may sometimes *feel* stuck or confused about your next move. Sometimes the obstacles may stop you in your tracks completely. You may feel helpless. (Though there are times that you can jump or drive right over *other* obstacles.)

Your obstacles can either break you or make you trust God more. You can trust that God is like a strong "rock" for you. He can help you respond well to your obstacles (or *bumps*!).

No matter what your obstacles are, it is important to remember that God can be a sturdy and strong frame for you.

You could pray something like:

> Dear God,
> I am so upset by my situation right now. I feel confused and upset by my obstacle. Help me to trust in You and Your strength. Help me to do right and not to get mad at others for what I am going through. Please help me to find a grown-up or friend who can help me to respond well and trust You during this hard time.
> Amen

Application Questions:

» What would a monster truck look like without a frame?

» Did any of the above life obstacles sound familiar to you? If not, what is an obstacle you are currently experiencing? (What is keeping you from doing what you want?)

» When obstacles arise, do you think you are like the *wise person* in your responses? (Do you want to obey what the Bible teaches, even when life is difficult?)

» Do you view God as a strong frame that can hold you up spiritually?

#4

Driving Point #4
MONSTER TRUCKS DO NOT HAVE
FULLY AIRED-UP TIRES.

Does your mom or dad (or older sibling) get a tad nervous when driving through a bumpy construction zone? Does your friend's parent slow down when driving on a road filled with potholes? Do any of these people worry about their tires in these bumpy circumstances?

It would never be wise to drive a normal vehicle wildly through rough stretches of any road. The vehicle's tires would not respond well to this type of adventure.

Thankfully, monster trucks do not have to rely on the same rules of the road! After all, monster truck rallies would be boring without the bumps, jumps, and wild landings.

There is one important reason that monster truck drivers can trust that their tires will survive a rough landing. Monster truck tires are not filled all the way with air! As a result, the tires are less likely to burst on a bumpy landing.

According to *The Monster Jam Official Guidebook*, Monster Jam's ® BKT-brand tires need to hold only twenty-three pounds of air pressure for the tires to be filled. Crazily, a normal car tire may have around thirty pounds of pressure.

Under the activities section on monsterjam.com, there is neat information under the "Truck Body Facts" section. It teaches that the ideal tire inflation for monster trucks is 23 PSI. With this ideal air pressure, mixed in with the strong BKT-brand tires, these monster trucks can have appropriate truck bounce.

As a result of the lower air pressure, monster truck tires can look deflated after a big landing. If someone did not know that this was okay (and that the tires were doing their job), the person could say, "*WOAH!*" or "*OH NO!*" and expect the tires to not survive. The monster truck tires perform quite well, though.

Of course, it is still possible that monster truck tires can pop. The wheels do survive more bouncy landings than not, though. This is because the tires are filled with just the *right* amount of air.

Bible Takeaway:

If you did not know about the purpose of monster truck tires not being aired up fully, would you have said, "*WOAH, OH NO!*" if you saw a monster truck land with its tire looking deflated on impact? This *WOAH* would be an *OKAY* thing, though, right?

In the same way, spiritually speaking, sometimes a difficulty seems like a really big "*WOAH, OH NO!*" Yet, God has His plan, and life's *bumps* and difficulties can actually be viewed as *OKAY*.

Let's look at a few Bible passages to help us work through this idea.

One of the most well-known men in the New Testament was the Apostle Paul. He was a traveling missionary who helped spread the truth of Jesus Christ. God used Paul to write many books of the New Testament.

Long story short, Paul was not always well-liked. Groups of people were often angry at him for preaching the truth about Jesus. Groups of men tried to beat up Paul and chase him out of their different towns. Paul was also arrested on several occasions for preaching.

In Acts 16, Paul and his helper (Silas) were beaten and thrown into prison. To me, this could easily be viewed as "*WOAH, not fair a bit!*" Paul and Silas did not deserve this treatment. However, Paul and Silas chose to keep a good attitude in their difficult circumstances. Here is what the Bible said that they did:

> Now about midnight Paul and Silas were praying and singing hymns of praise to God... (Acts 16:25a)

While in prison, they prayed and sang to God.

Paul's life did not get any easier! At the end of the book of Acts, here are some of the shocking things that happened to him (just for preaching about Jesus):

- He was arrested by an angry mob (Acts 21:26-36).

- A group of forty men formed a pact to kill him (Acts 23:12-13).

- People wanted to trick Paul and ambush him (Acts 25:1-4).

- Leaders brought Paul to be charged for crimes that they could not even prove (Acts 25:6-8).

- He was in a shipwreck (Acts 27:39-41).

- Once on dry land again, a snake bit him (Acts 28:3).

- He was put under house arrest for two years (Acts 28).

These could be considered truly *WOAH* moments! Here is where things become interesting, though.

Paul did not fight God's plan. In fact, when Paul was stuck in his house under arrest (with a guard always near), Paul wrote an encouraging book in the New Testament.

After Paul had such *bumpy* trials, he still was willing to write the book of Philippians. I encourage you to read through Philippians 4. Paul wrote about joy and contentment. He included verses on prayer and the promised peace of God.

How incredible!

Application:

Think of a variety of possible stressful things for your age group. Next, think of extremely exciting things for your age group.

If you asked the same-age children in your circle of friends to do the same, would everyone have the same answers?

Some things in life seem more stressful or extreme to one person, but not necessarily to another (and vice versa).

For example, losing a big championship game may not be a big deal to one friend. Perhaps it is very stressful for another friend, though. Maybe your other friend would stress if he had to write a story for English class, but it would not bother you.

The point is that some things in life are *WOAH* moments for you, yet *OKAY* for others. Sometimes life may seem as if the hard times could deflate you. Do trials seemingly "take the air out of you" at times?

This is when it is important to take God at His word. It is important to trust God and His plan for you. He gives us strength and help. He can help you keep joy during difficult times.

I learned a neat concept from a pastor's wife who is also a church children's teacher. Her name is Emily Woodlee. She teaches that you and your friends can *believe in God*, yet it is also important to just *believe God* and remember to apply the promises He has given in the Bible.

Application Questions:

» Are you in a difficult situation that stresses you out more than it stresses out your friends? (Is something *WOAH* to you but *OKAY* for others?)

» On the other hand, what feels *WOAH* to one of your friends but *OKAY* to you?

» What shocked you the most about what happened to the Apostle Paul in the New Testament?

» I encourage you to write the following on an index card, journal, or piece of paper: *I can believe in God, but I should also believe God!*

#5

Driving Point #5

What is something challenging for you? Is it a particular sport, math class, reading, or just figuring out a new video game that your friend showed you? Does it ever annoy you when a parent or teacher encourages you to *just persevere*? What does that even mean, right?

I tell my children that persevering is *doing what is hard, even when you do not feel like it*. Perhaps this definition is a little too basic. Yet, persevering is simply the act of continuing to work hard (even when it is difficult or annoyingly *bumpy*) to meet a particular goal.

Monster truck drivers must persevere to reach individual driving goals. Each driver's goal may be slightly different. Some may desire to work hard to win a major competition. Others may work hard to qualify to be a part of a specific rally. The point is, that if there is a personal goal, then perseverance becomes necessary.

In the book, *Fly Guy Presents Monster Trucks*, the author wrote that at times, it may take monster truck drivers several years to learn stunts. Several years sound discouraging to me. Yet, a good driver must not give up if he or she desires to enter the big competitions.

I enjoyed interviewing Monster Jam ® driver, Brianna Mahon. She drives the WHIPLASH truck. She shared neat information with me about her need to persevere in a unique way.

Brianna went to Monster Jam University ® which involves intense training for the Monster Jam ® drivers. For Brianna, her biggest obstacle to work through at the university was the media training. She admits she was a very shy person. The idea of having to put herself in front of the news media and other people was *terrifying*. Public speaking was never *her thing*.

She had to persevere to overcome her fear of speaking in front of crowds (sometimes of 80,000 people!). With all the practice— even when she may not have felt like it—she is now able to be more at ease while doing interviews with news or radio stations and television shows. She admits that now she can do live interviews as if she had been doing them all her life.

I appreciated Brianna's honesty in this area of perseverance. Had she refused to do this portion of Monster Jam University ® training, she may not have been successful to reach her goal of being a Monster Jam ® driver. For her, she had to keep her eye on the prize. This "prize" of being a Monster Jam ® driver involved the uncomfortable practice of learning to be interviewed.

Bible Takeaway:
THERE IS A NEED TO PERSEVERE IN THE MIDDLE OF LIFE'S *BUMPS*.

Grown-ups will encourage you to persevere. They will often say, "Keep trying! You will catch on!"

I get it; this can get annoying. When something is frustrating, difficult, or maddening, the last thing you want to hear is to *keep trying*. Sometimes, you may feel so exhausted and annoyed at life that you have zero strength left to attempt any more hard work!

How can the Bible be encouraging in this topic?

In the Old Testament, Isaiah wrote about tired and exhausted youth and how sometimes they fail. Isaiah also wrote about the strength and power of God.

Here are a few of the parts from Isaiah 40:

> **Do you not know? Have you not heard? The Everlasting God, the LORD, the Creator of the ends of the earth does not become weary or tired. His understanding is unsearchable. He gives strength to the weary, and to the one who lacks might, He increases power. Though youths grow weary and tired, and vigorous young men stumble badly, yet those who wait for the LORD will gain new strength... (Isaiah 40:28-31a)**

These verses are honest and to-the-point. There will be times that you will fail or have difficulty moving forward through some life difficulty based on *your personal* strength. These are brutal thoughts, aren't they?

There is also encouragement found in these verses, though. You are promised to have <u>God's strength</u> in your life's *bumps*. God never, ever, ever gets tired! He is always available to offer you strength when your days become too stressful.

The idea of *waiting for the LORD* (verse 31) has to do with patient hope in God and His plan for your life. There is great importance in remembering God's promises. He promises to be with you and give you the necessary strength in difficult times.

Here is one more quick look back at the Apostle Paul in the New Testament. Remember all his stresses from the last *Bible Takeaway*?

In the New Testament, Paul wrote the following about his circumstances.

> **At my first defense no one supported me, but all deserted me; may it not be counted against them. But the Lord stood with me and strengthened me... (2 Timothy 4:16-17a)**

Paul lost friends and seemingly had no support through parts of his missionary journeys. People failed him. God never failed him, though. God gave Paul strength in life, even when people made his life difficult.

Application:

You may understandably wonder why this information is even in a perseverance section. I know it is hard to keep trying when you are guaranteed to experience difficulties. There are times I wish life was easier!

The one thing you can hold on to is the fact that God loves you and will give you the necessary strength when life is overly frustrating and difficult.

Here are two examples:

> What if you were told you could finally join a new robotics club? You were so excited until you realized it was much more difficult than you imagined. Let's pretend that a parent encouraged

you to stay in it for at least a month. You wanted to stay in the club but were overwhelmed each week. One thing you could do is pray that God would give you the strength to keep a good attitude and to keep the desire to do your best, even when it became extra hard!

Pretend you were in a new gymnastics class that required more flexibility than you had at the time. There were many new (and difficult) skills to learn. Others caught on more quickly than you, and you became frustrated and upset. Though you desired to learn, you were not sure that you could keep your frustration under control. You could pray that God would calm your mind and give you the strength to try your hardest (with the right attitude). He can give you the strength to choose to do your best and not worry about other classmates' performance in class.

God never expects perfection! He desires you to do your best and pray to Him for the help you need to keep trying, even when it gets hard. That is perseverance at its best. You do not have to do anything with your own strength.

Application Questions:

» Is there an area of life in which it is difficult to persevere?

» Which part of Isaiah 40:28-31a encourages you the most?

» What is happening in life that is currently taking away your strength? I encourage you to stop right now and take your worries to God in prayer. Ask God to give you the necessary strength that only HE can give.

» How can you persevere just *a little more* in a specific area? (God can give you the strength to keep going, even when it is hard.)

#6

Driving Point #6

Do you enjoy roller coasters (or no way!)? They can swerve, jolt, spin, and whip you around! Roller coasters are not for everyone.

In my interview with Monster Jam ® driver, Brianna Mahon, she stated that driving a monster truck is similar to riding a roller coaster. She acknowledged that the adrenaline rush between riding a roller coaster and driving a monster truck is a lot alike.

Brianna has raced, jumped, and competed in other events for her whole life. Long before her monster truck days, she was more accustomed to the jolts of such events compared to what others may be.

She thought back, though, to the first time she ever drove a monster truck. She *felt* as if she were going so high and fast. It was not until she watched the video that she realized she was not going as fast or as high as she first thought! It was as if her body was playing tricks on her.

Brianna admitted that she does sometimes get dizzy in a "donut competition." She compared it to being on a merry-go-round. She said that the dizzy feeling does improve after a few seconds, though.

Bible Takeaway:
LIFE CAN BE JOLTING AND DIZZYING AT TIMES!
REMEMBER WHO IS ALWAYS WITH YOU.

The Bible is jam-packed with jolting and dizzying life situations! You have already seen the New Testament example of the Apostle Paul. Let's consider an Old Testament example of a man named Joseph.

Joseph was the favorite son of his father, Jacob. Joseph's brothers were jealous of him being the favorite. They could not stand Joseph.

Here are some of the jolting things that happened to Joseph ("thanks" to his brothers and others).

- Joseph's brothers wanted to kill him (Genesis 37:18).

- Instead, they threw him into a pit (Genesis 37:22-24).

- The brothers then decided to sell Joseph into slavery, and Joseph was taken to Egypt (Genesis 37:27-29).

- While in Egypt, Joseph's master's wife told lies about him and Joseph was thrown wrongly into prison (Genesis 39:19-20).

God was with Joseph, though. Joseph was eventually released from prison and put in leadership under Egypt's ruler. God used Joseph to rescue that part of the world from the effects of drought and famine.

Joseph was even able to rescue his brothers, without them knowing who he was at the time. Amazingly, Joseph's brothers eventually found out it was their brother (Joseph) who rescued them.

> They were then fearful of how much power Joseph had in Egypt. (Genesis 45:3)

Joseph could have had them killed.

Instead, Joseph forgave them and told them not to be fearful. In fact, Joseph promised to provide for their needs (Genesis 50:18-21).

Joseph never gave up. How could Joseph keep going and trust God in such jolting circumstances? Joseph knew that God was with him and would strengthen him to survive each day.

> And the LORD was with Joseph...Now his master saw that the LORD was with him... (Genesis 39:2a, 3a)

> But the LORD was with Joseph and extended kindness to him, and gave him favor in the sight of the warden of the prison...because the LORD was with him; and, the LORD made whatever he did prosper. (Genesis 39:21, 23b)

Joseph's brothers brought many jolts into Joseph's life! Joseph's life situations were dizzying for sure. Yet, God was always with him (just like with the Bible promises we have already seen in this book).

Application:

Some things in life are much more dizzying to one person than another. For example, when my family attended our county's monster truck rally, we rode on the special "monster truck ride" that audience members can pay to ride. It probably lasted only 2 ½ minutes.

I thought I was going to get sick or pass out. It was horrible for me! The other people on the ride, though, did not seem to be phased nearly as much. With the simple tricks this driver was doing, it was a tad embarrassing that I could hardly handle the basic moves (especially if monster truck drivers could handle many more spins, jumps, and turns than **my** *simple* ride).

Quite honestly, there was NOTHING simple about that ride for me, though! In the same way in life, some difficulties (or trials) are much more difficult for someone to handle than for another. This is okay!

You may be *jolted* by being told you cannot play in your championship sports game because you must travel to a funeral with your family.

It may be *dizzying* to you if you were told you must stand in front of your class at school to give a presentation. Maybe it is *dizzying* if you are asked to read a story in front of your class at church.

It is possible to be jolted by being told you would have to move to a new state and leave your friends behind. What about a car accident or a special family member who gets sick?

There is nothing wrong with you if you are *jolted* or *dizzy* by something that does not bother another person. There will be difficult times that genuinely affect YOU. I encourage you to remember Who never leaves you during the *bumpy* points in your life.

God is always there for you. For this reason, you and your friends can find the strength to keep going!

Application Questions:

» Would you dare to ride in a Monster Jam truck with Brianna Mahon during her freestyle competition, if only there was a spot for a passenger? Yes, or no way?

» In the world's eyes, was Joseph's life *fair*? Did he *deserve* all the hardships (and the *jolts*)?

» Joseph's brothers were jealous of Joseph. As a result, what were some of the wrong choices the brothers made?

» Genesis 39 states many times how the LORD was with Joseph. Try to either write down one of the verses or highlight each of the Bible verses when each statement is found in Genesis 39.

Driving Point #7

What is your favorite part of monster truck rallies? Do you enjoy watching them because of the wheelies, races, or fancy trick competitions? Perhaps it is all the above!

You and the audience (whether watching in-person or on some form of technology) love the excitement of the engines revving and the trucks flying high. There are other people, though, whose main jobs have nothing to do with watching an exciting show.

Track officials have two main jobs. The first job is to keep the drivers, crew, and audience safe. Secondly, the officials make sure the rules are being followed.

For safety's sake, track officials have the authority and ability to force monster trucks to shut off if there is any potential danger. At any point, the officials can use a "Remote Ignition Interrupter" (RII) to shut off any of the monster trucks at the rally. This RII works like a remote control.

When my family was at a WGAS Motorsports' monster truck rally, I saw one of the monster trucks get shut down by an official. The truck was getting too close to one of the walls. As a result, one of the officials automatically powered down the truck.

What if this driver disagreed with the official? Yelling at the official would not earn the driver any points. The desire to fight the official's choice may even get the driver disqualified from that competition or kicked out of the rally altogether.

The official gets to make the final call about shutting down a truck or not. One of the official's main goals is safety, not just allowing the crowd to see the most exciting show.

Officials also make sure each of the drivers is following the rules. Cheating or unfair play removes the fun for all. Track officials are necessary, even if it is hard to agree with them on *every* decision they make.

Bible Takeaway:
THERE ARE IMPORTANT "TRACK OFFICIALS" WHO HAVE AUTHORITY IN YOUR LIFE.

The main goals of the track officials are to provide *safety* and a *fair* rally. Neither the audience nor crew members want injuries *or* cheating during the monster truck competitions.

The same holds true for those who have leadership and authority in your life.

The Bible has helpful verses to help explain the importance of obeying your parents. Your parents could be considered the most important "track officials" in your life.

In the book of Proverbs, King Solomon reminded his child to pay attention to his rules. He gave two specific purposes for obedience—peace, and safety.

My son, do not forget my teaching, but have your heart comply with my commandments; for length of days and years of life and peace they will add to you. (Proverbs 3:1-2)

Solomon knew that obedience brought a safer and more peace-filled life.

Ephesians 6:1-3 teaches the same concept. Life goes much easier when you obey your "track officials."

Though other people in your life could be considered "track officials," let's consider the Highest of all—the Creator God.

The Old Testament book Ecclesiastes ends with a powerful statement:

The conclusion, when everything has been heard, is: fear God and keep His commandments, because this applies to every person. (Ecclesiastes 12:13)

This verse means that each of us needs to trust and obey God's way. Let's keep in mind that those who are in authority are there to help us be safe and have peace.

Application:

Sometimes you may disagree with your parent's choice. Honestly, I disagreed with the track official at the monster truck rally my family attended. In my opinion, the monster truck was not close enough to the wall for the official to automatically shut off the truck.

In the long run, my opinion did not matter. That official had more experience than I did, and that official was given the authority to make the choice, not me!

Parents do not always make choices that will make you happiest. You may not always understand why they say *no* or *wait*, but thankfully the Bible gives the benefits of responding well to those in authority.

Let's look at the following "made-up" scenario, but from the "wrong perspective."

> Pretend you have twin friends named Billy and Shay Walker. What if these friends' parents told Billy and Shay not to attend Jacob's party. Mr. and Mrs. Walker were not sure Jacob's parents were in town. They did not feel there would be enough adult supervision.
>
> What if Billy chose to sneak out to attend the party? What if Shay lied and said she was going to another friend's house but instead went to Jacob's party? Unfortunately, this is what they chose to do.
>
> Once getting there, Billy and Shay quickly realized that Jacob's party was not what they expected. The only "adults" there were Jacob's teenage brother and sister. The party was loud and chaotic. Some of the older children were making unwise choices.
>
> Billy and Shay wanted to leave, but then their parents would find out that they lied and sneaked around. What would they do?
>
> Billy called Mr. Walker, and both children were picked up from the party. At home, the Walkers told Billy and Shay that they were not to go to that party because there was no way to know for sure

the activities would be safe without proper adult supervision.

Plus, because Billy and Shay lied, they would have consequences. They would lose out on the opportunity to go to the amusement park with their aunt and uncle that weekend. Billy was mad. Shay was shocked. They had no peace that night because of their disobedience.

Their parents told them that obedience brings peace and safety. They wanted to protect <u>and</u> offer their children peace. Obedience was the path to both.

Think back to the last time you disobeyed. Was there a lack of peace as a result? Was there the potential for danger?

Doing things God's way will keep you and your friends on the right track. Of course, good obedience does not mean you will never have difficulties in life. Unfortunately, trials sometimes strike, for no understandable reason. Yet, if you show a lifestyle of obedience, your path will not have needless stress and pain.

Application Questions:

» What are the two main purposes of track officials?

» Who are some of the main "track officials" that God has placed in your life?

» Do you have *room for improvement* on how you respect your personal "track officials?"

» According to the Bible verses we looked at (Proverbs 3:1-2 and Ephesians 6:1-3), what are the two main benefits of obedience?

#8

Driving Point #8
MONSTER TRUCK DRIVERS NEED HELP FROM OTHER EXPERTS.

When you are in a difficult situation, the words, "Help is on the way!" may be music to your ears.

What about monster trucks? What happens when the trucks lose a tire or any other important part? What if the engines need major fixing or the trucks flip upside down completely? It must be nice for the drivers to hear, "Help is on the way!"

There are different types of experts on which monster truck drivers must rely. First, drivers must rely on and trust their crew.

Crew members must be well-trained. This makes them the experts in their fields. I enjoyed learning from a Monster Jam ® Crew Chief. He obtained two degrees and a diploma from the University of Northwestern Ohio (UNOH). This Crew Chief said that he was able to receive the skills needed to be successful in both the monster truck and motorsport industries.

Brianna Mahon shared with me the value of being able to trust each crew member as a person *and* as a mechanic. Her safety is important, and she understands the importance to feel comfortable within her truck. Having a crew who she can fully trust provides this comfort.

Though Brianna is mechanically inclined and can help problem-solve truck issues, she ultimately knows that the crew must take care of everything. She leaves that to them.

These technicians can include welders, mechanics, and all-things problem solvers.

I mentioned the "UNOH Pit Report" in a previous Driving Point. That rally was from 2020. Reporters Scott Jordan, Bari Musawwir, and Casey Gagliardi were discussing how one of the drivers needed to get mechanical work done during the rally. Casey Gagliardi explained that there was no need to worry about the driver seeking out mechanical help. She said it was common to have to readjust the truck's settings when moving from one competition to another. The drivers must be willing to trust their mechanical crew to do what is best for the team.

As a team, drivers and their crew also can "eye-ball the track." MonsterJam.com mentions that drivers and their crew check out the track before a rally so that they can get a feel for the track and its parts. They can then make good plans for the rally.

The drivers must also be willing to receive help from experts outside of their normal *team*. This help could be from the drivers of heavy construction equipment. These machines hook up to the monster trucks if the monster trucks get completely stuck or flipped. Help could also come from a team of firefighters who help put out a dangerous fire during a race.

Bible Takeaway:

GOD HAS PLACED NEEDED "EXPERTS" IN YOUR LIFE.

If monster truck drivers need help on the field, they do not just go ask some random person in the crowd for help. The drivers know they must go to the *right sources* for help.

The Bible has good advice about *where* to receive advice and help in life.

1. Go directly to God in prayer when you need wisdom or direction.

Trust in the LORD with all your heart and do not lean on your own understanding. In all your ways acknowledge Him, and He will make your paths straight.
PROVERBS 3:5-6

The Bible teaches that you should not lean on your own understanding—especially because life can be filled with confusion at times. Instead, you can lean into God and pay attention to His words in the Bible to help keep you on the right path in life.

2. Pay attention to your parents' instructions.

Listen, my son, to your father's instruction, and do not ignore your mother's teaching.
PROVERBS 1:8

Even though parents can sure seem *uncool* or out to ruin all sorts of your fun, the Bible teaches that you should listen to (not ignore!) what your parents are telling you. God has designed for them to help you figure out life choices.

3. Pay attention to all wise advice.

A wise person will hear and increase in learning, and a person of understanding will acquire wise counsel.
PROVERBS 1:5

Notice the fifth word, *hear.* It is valuable to truly listen to good advice. The second half of this verse is encouraging you to get *wise* counsel. This type of advice is designed to help you make choices. Wise counsel (though perhaps not what you *want* to hear at any given time) is never designed to hurt you or mislead you. Wise counsel will always have the goal to benefit you.

Much of Proverbs deals with how to be wise. True wisdom comes when someone desires to do things God's way (by following the Bible).

4. Stay away from *bad company*!

Do not be deceived: "Bad company corrupts good morals."
1 CORINTHIANS 15:33

It is never helpful to hang out with the wrong crowd! The wrong crowd will get you into trouble AND wrongly influence you to have bad values and character. Never let those with bad character be your "experts" for you when you have a problem to work through in life.

Think of a rotten apple or banana. These are corrupt and messed-up foods! You do not want to have rotten or messed-up character traits in life because of the friends with whom you hang out.

Application:

There will certainly be times in life when you will need help from good and reliable "experts." Do you know who you can go to if you need an "expert" to help you through life's situations?

There are a variety of specific people that God has placed in your life to help you make choices.

Though it can be hard at times, trust that your parents are "experts" that you can go to for help. They know you and your situation the best. They desire to help you, no matter how frustrating their ideas seem at the time.

What if a monster truck had engine trouble during a race? What if the driver was mad at his crew chief because they argued about a few things before the rally started? Would it be wise or foolish for the driver to refuse truck advice from the crew chief because of the earlier argument?

In the same way, you will sometimes be frustrated with your parents. They still want what is best for you, even if you just argued. They are still "experts" in your life who truly want to lead you on the right path.

There will be times in life when you will seek advice from other "experts." It is a blessing to have other trusted friends and grown-ups help you through life's choices. Just be sure their lifestyle and advice will not cause you to become like *rotten* fruit in your character.

Most of all, though, allow Bible principles to be your guide when making life decisions. Seek out people in your life who will point you to make decisions that will please God. Then, you will know for sure that you are receiving wise advice.

Application Questions:

» Who are some of the needed and valuable experts for each Monster Jam team?

» Are there specific things that you purposely or wrongly ignore from a wise *expert* in your life? (As a result, how do things typically turn out?)

» Do you hang out with any friends who could negatively impact your character? Is there a grownup in your life whom you could ask for help to figure out how to deal with this "friend problem?"

» Write down a list of wise experts that God has placed in your life. Keep this list handy when you have a problem that requires some expert grownup help.

#9

Driving Point #9
MONSTER TRUCK DRIVERS MUST BE PREPARED.

Have you ever been on vacation and wished you had packed *that one thing*? Maybe it was a spare bathing suit or your favorite sandals. Perhaps it was your favorite book or that new set of colored pens and paper for the car ride.

It is safe to say that monster truck drivers do not desire to have that *"bummer-I-forgot..."* moment! Though these drivers are very talented and perform the fancy tricks that excite the fans, they know there are certain things they must not forget. There is much safety preparation that happens behind the scenes (and before any of the audience steps foot inside an arena).

Yes, the drivers must be prepared. In general, though, the drivers, teams, and track officials must be ready in the area of safety. Thankfully, even before monster truck rallies start, the safety of drivers is carefully planned in proactive ways.

Specifically, proactive care can be given to the scrap cars (also called *crush cars*) used in certain rallies. Before these types of rallies take place, the workers take out the scrap cars' fuel, batteries, and glass. These would be dangerous items to have scattered around the monster rally floor.

The Monster Jam Guidebook explains other safety mechanisms for the drivers and monster trucks:

1. THE DRIVERS' SEATS ARE CUSTOM-MADE TO FIT EACH SPECIFIC DRIVER. PLUS, A FIVE-POINT HARNESS IS INCLUDED TO KEEP THE DRIVERS HELD SECURELY INTO THEIR PROTECTIVE PLACE.

2. MONSTER TRUCKS ALSO HAVE A SAFETY "CUT-OFF SWITCH" INSIDE THE CABS. THE DRIVERS CAN USE THIS SWITCH TO STOP THE TRUCKS IN AN EMERGENCY.

3. EACH PIECE OF THE DRIVER'S SUIT IS FIRE-RESISTANT. THIS INCLUDES THEIR GLOVES AND SHOES.

The monster truck drivers come to the rally to fly high and wow the crowd. Yet, they also know that with such excitement comes the potential for true danger. The drivers and teams use great wisdom when they come prepared.

Bible Takeaway:

As seen above, monster truck drivers need a variety of protections to stay safe. Did you know that there are spiritual protections available, too? Since there are spiritual temptations to do wrong or to respond badly in tough circumstances, there is "spiritual armor" to help Christians (also called *the children of God*) make wise and obedient choices.

In Ephesians 6, the Apostle Paul wrote about protective armor to protect soldiers. Specifically, Paul used examples of the Roman soldier armor from the timeframe when the New Testament was written. Paul then applied the concept of physical armor to spiritual armor.

Just as the Roman soldiers needed armor for physical protection, children of God need spiritual armor to protect them in spiritual areas.

Pastor MacArthur has written helpful information to understand this concept of armor a little bit more. The list of armor is found in Ephesians 6:13-17. There are six specific pieces listed. The examples of physical armor are bolded. The examples of the spiritual armor are underlined.

1. **Belt** of Truth
2. **Breastplate** of Righteousness
3. **Shoes** put on with the Gospel of Peace
4. **Shield** of Faith
5. **Helmet** of Salvation
6. **Sword** of the Spirit (Bible)

I will not list all the possible details about each of these. An entire book could be written on each one. I will only include some of the highlights.

The Roman soldiers would have used the following armor when in battle. This way, the soldiers were always prepared for danger. The soldiers knew that danger could strike at any time.

- The soldiers' belts would hold back any clothing that could get in the way. Plus, these belts could help hold other necessities for battle.
- The soldiers wore protective breastplates to cover their hearts and other vital organs.

- The soldiers wore special shoes. These would provide more traction so the shoes could grip the ground better during battle.
- The soldiers used shields to protect their whole bodies when they were under attack.
- The soldiers' helmets were necessary to give extra protection to their heads and brains when the enemies were striking.
- The soldiers held swords to defend themselves from danger and attack the enemies.

In a physical war, there are many necessary pieces of armor to protect soldiers. The Apostle Paul taught about spiritual armor, too. Children of God need spiritual help to overcome temptations to do wrong things.

Spiritual armor can help the children of God in the following ways:

- They help the children of God understand they can trust in God for salvation. God can also be trusted to give strength to help them respond well in difficult situations.
- Through this armor, children of God can know about the best path/choice in life (by obeying what the Bible teaches).
- This spiritual armor provides stability and peace when life gets difficult.
- The spiritual weapon—the Bible—can help children of God defeat sinful temptations.

The armor listed in Ephesians 6 helps compare the importance of physical armor and spiritual armor. It is important to be prepared for spiritual temptations and discouragements. The best way to make it through such difficulties is to trust God for His strength and obey what the Bible teaches.

Application:

Some of the above soldier discussions may have been a tad confusing. Here is the takeaway for you personally. You will sometimes experience *bumps* and sadness. You will experience temptations to get mad when life does not go your way.

The best way to defend yourself during these situations is to be prepared spiritually. Specifically, it becomes important for you to know specific Bible verses to help you overcome specific temptations.

For example, let's pretend you know you are often tempted to complain or argue when you are asked to do something you do not like. For you, spiritual armor might be memorizing the following Bible verse:

**Do all things without complaining or arguments.
(Philippians 2:14)**

Perhaps you are tempted to lie when you are afraid you will get in trouble for something. Using spiritual armor could cause you to think about the section in Proverbs that teaches about how God hates lying. (See Proverbs 6:16-19.)

If you struggle with making wise choices about who your friends are, you could think about verses like Proverbs 1:10, 1:15, 4:14-15, 22:3, and 27:12. These Proverbs teach the major importance of staying away from those who cause trouble. The verses teach the importance of keeping away from evil altogether. If your friends are always tempting you to do wrong, spiritual armor may help you understand that it is time to find some new friends.

Spiritual armor is not designed to keep you from fun. It is designed to protect you from making choices that could either harm you or take your peace.

Application Questions:

» Which monster truck safety feature is the most interesting to you?

» What piece of spiritual armor sounds the most important to you?

» Have you trusted God to save you from your sins? (If you are curious to learn more about this, I have included a section at the back of this book to tell you how you can become a child of God.)

» The spiritual weapon (the Bible) helps a child of God to defeat temptations. What Bible verse can you find that can help you to make better choices during a temptation?

#10

Driving Point #10

When you were a young child, I have a feeling you often asked a parent or grandparent if you were getting bigger or heavier. Your parent or grandparent would certainly know the answer, as you would become more and more difficult to hold. With growing weight comes the excitement that you are indeed getting older.

In the monster truck world, though, heavy is not always the ideal thing. In fact, monster truck parts need to be light (yet still strong).

To stay on the lighter side, the *body* of monster trucks is made of fiberglass. Fiberglass is made up of glass and plastic and is much lighter than metal.

These lighter parts allow the drivers to take their trucks higher and faster. The lighter parts do not hinder the trucks' strength, though. These strong trucks can still crush cars. The light parts are important to help the drivers perform their tricks more efficiently.

Even the tires play a role in the overall desired weight. Small portions of each tire can be shaved away to prepare the truck for a race. This small change helps the trucks weigh less.

In my non-technical way of thinking, this small tire change seems like a lot of work. The experts view it as beneficial, though, as small changes are worth it to the drivers.

Remember: less weight for monster trucks equals higher and more exciting jumps! These high-flying jumps are what please the crowd and keep them coming back for more action.

Bible Takeaway:
WHEN YOU FEEL WEIGHED DOWN WITH STRESS, CAST YOUR WORRIES TO GOD!

Monster trucks are heavy, but they benefit from lighter parts when possible. As mentioned above, the trucks can then fly higher, right?

Sometimes in life, you may feel *weighed down* by the difficulties of life. Trials can seem like heavy weights, which make life harder to understand. These life *bumps* are frustrating, too!

The Bible shares helpful thoughts on how to deal with these hard trials.

King David wrote many Psalms in the Old Testament about being weighed down with stress and fear. Yet, he often shared how he relied on God to strengthen him in the hard times.

Psalm 55 is a great example of how King David worked through his difficulties in life. The Psalm shows that King David was stressed. Enemies were out to get him. He was overwhelmed and fearful. He wrote this interesting verse.

> I said, "Oh, that I had wings like a dove!
> I would fly away and be at rest". (Psalm 55:6)

David wished he could have his weight of stress lifted so that he could fly away from his troubles and then have rest.

> At the end of this Psalm, though, King David stated the importance of casting his burdens onto God. David wrote, "Cast your burden upon the LORD and He will sustain you..." (Psalm 55:22a)

Casting your burden means that you can pray and throw your concerns over to God. The result is that God will uplift you and allow you to survive your difficult times.

The concept of *casting your burden* is also found in the New Testament.

> Having cast all your anxiety on Him,
> because He cares about you. (1 Peter 5:7)

When life seems too heavy and difficult, your heavy burdens in life can be lightened. God cares about your needs and stresses. He is available to help you make it through your trials. You can pray to God for strength. His strength can help make your stresses seem *lighter*.

Application:

Imagine if you came inside from playing in the snow, you would probably want to "throw off" your winter coat if you sat by a fireplace.

Pretend you just changed out of your wet bathing suit and had on your favorite dry clothes again. If your friend jokingly threw your wet pool towel on your shoulders, would you not quickly throw off this wet towel?

The idea of "casting" your care and burden on God is similar to this "throwing off" concept. Sometimes you will have stresses and concerns in life that will weigh you down emotionally. You can figuratively throw these burdens off your shoulder. Throw them to God, *in prayer*!

Maybe the big achievement test in school weighs you down. Perhaps having to pack up and move to a different home stresses you out. What if you are stuck with a health problem that will last your whole life?

These can be truly stressful and heavy-feeling events. Thankfully, God tells you that you can *throw* your burdens onto Him by praying.

An example prayer could be:

> God, I am facing a really hard situation. It is scary and frustrating. Please help me to do what is right even in my hard time. Help give me the strength to make it through this problem. I want to trust You to help me survive this situation. I cast my problems onto You. Please help me.
>
> Amen

Remember how monster truck tires are slightly shaved to make the truck even lighter. I love this concept. Even *small* changes help the truck weigh less.

Spiritually speaking, small changes in your level of faith can help your burdens weigh less. Trusting God's plan AND His promise of strength can make a big difference in your life.

Application Questions:

» Are you experiencing a current hardship in life that seems too heavy to bear on your own?

» Have you ever wanted to run away from your *bumps* in life? King David wanted to fly away from his! (See Psalm 55:6.)

» Instead of running away, I encourage you to read Psalm 55:22a. Can you cast your hardship to God in prayer? You can pray the example prayer that is listed just a few paragraphs above.

» To help lighten your stress in life, what small (yet still valuable) change can you make in your level of faith in God? (Can you ask a church worker to show you an encouraging Bible verse? Can you make a reminder to pray first thing each morning?)

MonsterJam.com

#11

Driving Point #11

MONSTER TRUCK SEATS ARE FITTED SPECIFICALLY TO THE DRIVER.

Have you ever been snow or water skiing? Have you ever worn bowling shoes or roller skates? Perhaps you have worn some sort of athletic gear that had to fit *just right* to be comfortable.

For monster truck drivers, they must fit *just right* in their drivers' seats. This perfect fit is not just for the sake of comfort (though I am sure comfort is appreciated). Fitting well is also important for the drivers' safety.

In my interview with Monster Jam ® driver Brianna Mahon, she taught me very interesting things about the custom seats in which drivers must be correctly fitted.

There is quite a detailed process to properly fit drivers in their seats. Here are two neat parts of the process.

1. DETAILED MEASUREMENT MUST TAKE PLACE.

Brianna compared the measuring process to someone being fitted for a tuxedo. The drivers must get measured from head to toe. The driver seats are then built to those specifications.

2. THE NEWLY-BUILT DRIVER SEAT COMES TO THE SHOP FOR THE FINAL (YET IMPORTANT) SAFETY DETAILS.

At this point in the process, the height of the head restraint must be properly set. Also, the rib supports of the chair are pushed in far enough. Foam is added to the sides and bottom of the chair. For this process, hot liquid is poured and dried *just right* to help the foam form to the specific curves of each driver. This dense foam can be shaved or cut to fit the driver perfectly.

In the end, Brianna mentioned how the finished seats must fit the drivers like a glove. There should be no gaps or spaces.

Bible Takeaway:

It is incredibly important that monster truck drivers fit well in their seats. These drivers are not responsible to fit well in the other driver's seats. Drivers must feel "at home" in their *own* seats!

In the same way, God desires His children to make something at home in their own lives, too.

Colossians 3:16a teaches, "Let the word of Christ richly dwell within you..."

Let's cover three main points from this short Bible section:

"WORD OF CHRIST"

There are a few ways to describe the *Word of Christ*. It deals with the Bible as a whole. You may have also heard the *Word of Christ* called the *Word of God* or *God's Word*.

Let's look at the next parts to see what to do with the *Word of Christ* (the Bible).

"DWELL"

Dwell deals with the idea of "making something at home."

If your grandma brought home a new plant, she would not just stuff it in her sock drawer, right? That would be ridiculous. She would be sure to know all about the specific type of plant she brought home. Does her plant need mostly sunlight during the day, or does her plant need time out of the sun? She would learn how much water her plant needs. She would probably put the plant where it would not get easily knocked over. Your grandma would make that plant be at *home*!

This is what God wants you to do with the Bible. He wants you to read Bible verses and make them "at home" in your heart. This means that you pay attention to the words and try your hardest to apply the Bible verses in your life situations.

"WITHIN YOU"

Here is where everything gets very specific. Just like drivers must fit their seats, you must have the Bible verses in YOUR heart. Forcing your friend to learn and apply a Bible verse will offer you no help in working through your own problems, right?

When life is hard, you can take the Word of Christ (the Bible) and make it be at home in your own heart.

Application:

Imagine that you have a classmate who always tries to bug you. Pretend this person sits behind you in class and enjoys kicking the legs of your chair. It is as if this person gets such joy in making you miserable.

You feel like crumpling up a piece of paper and throwing it at this person behind you. Plus, you want to shout mean names at him because you are so annoyed. Then, you stop before following through with your desires. It is because you remember the Bible verse that your Sunday school teacher taught:

> Let no unwholesome word come out of your mouth...Be kind to one another, compassionate, forgiving each other, just as God in Christ also has forgiven you. (Ephesians 4:29a, 32)

In that instant, you successfully allowed God's Word to *dwell* in your *own* heart! You took the Bible verse and applied it in that stressful moment. You chose to not shout and throw a wad of paper. Instead, you applied a Bible verse to make the right choice.

You do not have to keep experiencing your classmate's wrongdoings without help, though. It is okay to let the teacher know. However, by applying Bible verses *in-the-moment*, you can choose to please God with <u>your</u> choices.

That is how to let the Bible dwell in your heart.

Application Questions:

» Picture yourself being fitted for a monster truck driver's seat. Would this be a fun process, or would it seem strange? (You would be thankful for the protection, though, I am sure!)

» Have you ever tried to wear your friend's shoes or your older sibling's outfit? What if the clothes were just too uncomfortable? Whose clothes need to fit YOU—yours or the other person's clothes?

» I cheer you on to memorize the following Bible verse: "*Let the word of Christ richly dwell within you...*" (Colossians 3:16a). Having the Word of God (the Bible) in your heart is one of the most important things your spiritual heart will ever hold.

» What specific Bible verse(s) can you make at home in your heart for when times get tough? What Bible verse(s) can you memorize to help keep you from unwise choices?

#12

Driving Point #12
MONSTER TRUCKS SOMETIMES GET DIRTY AND MESSED UP!

Are you someone who jumps into any event without any fear of getting muddy or grass-stained? On the other hand, does the thought of getting dirty stress you out?

Monster trucks are guaranteed to get dirty *and* messed up from their jumps, races, and spins.

Here is the reason why the trucks have no hope to stay clean during rallies. Dump trucks bring in about 7,500 TONS of dirt onto the track for Monster Jam ® rallies. That is a lot of dirt.

Dump trucks and front loaders team up to get the course ready. When their jobs are done, other trucks spray water on the field before the rally starts. The wet course allows the monster trucks to have better traction.

Thanks to their big tires, monster trucks can drive through deep mud. I think it is safe to say that monster trucks are bound to get dirty during each rally.

One of the questions I asked the Monster Jam ® Crew Chief was about the dirtiness at rallies. He told me about the importance of the monster trucks' air filters. These filters help to keep the dirt out of the engines. Between the filters and the body of the engine, he told me that he then does not have to worry too much about the dirt or mud getting into the engine area.

Not only do these powerful trucks get dirty, but they also get a bit messed up on their bodies. Monster trucks flip and crush (and sometimes crash!).

This Crew Chief told me the importance of the trucks' bodies being made from fiberglass. Fiberglass is easier to repair. It is easier to fix the look of the fiberglass versus if the body was made from steel.

Sure, some repairs can happen behind the scenes at the rally, though other repairs must take place after the rally is done. The trucks are fixable, though.

Bible Takeaway:

EVEN WHEN YOU GET SPIRITUALLY DIRTY AND MESSED UP, GOD CAN FORGIVE YOU AND USE YOU AGAIN!

When monster trucks get dirty and messed up, wise drivers do not quit and angrily leave the rally. The crew members must not give up and go home without the desire to make the necessary repairs when possible. After all, monster trucks are fixable and usable, even if it takes longer to repair than desired.

Life can seem ugly sometimes. In this ugliness, sometimes you may fail and make mistakes. At times, you will have responses that do not please God.

Thankfully, God does not throw you aside as unusable!

Did you know that God's special chosen King of Israel made horrible life choices? King David did shocking things in the time of the Old Testament.

He took Bathsheba, another man's wife. Then, David tricked Bathsheba's husband and caused this man's death in battle. In the end, David married Bathsheba (2 Samuel 11).

In this dramatic set of events, King David made sinful choices. Yet, in Psalm 51, King David did important and brave things.

He admitted he sinned. Though he had done wrong, he did not make excuses. He asked God to "clean him" from his sinful choices. God was completely willing to forgive him. King David was still useable!

Application:

When you mess up and make unwise choices, you are not ruined for life. You are fixable and forgivable.

Let's pretend the following:

> Your parents told you that you will have a babysitter on Friday evening. You are allowed to eat the leftover pizza but not any of the chocolate cake on the counter.
>
> That evening, your babysitter had to make a quick phone call. Since she had no idea how much cake was there in the first place, she would never know

that you sneaked a quick piece. You were able to finish it just in time. You even had time to hide the plate and fork in the trashcan.

Your parents arrived back home later that evening, and you said goodbye to your babysitter. At bedtime, though, you felt bad. Plus, you felt itchy.

You developed a bad rash. You had to show your parents. Your mother was quite sad. She knew exactly what happened. She then told you that the chocolate cake had coconut flakes in it. You are allergic to coconut. Your parents certainly figured out that you were disobedient.

Thankfully, you felt bad about your wrong choice. You genuinely apologized, too. Though you had to live with the consequences, your parents willingly forgave you.

Your rash would go away, and you would still be a usable and loved part of your family.

Though the above situation was made-up, you still must seek forgiveness in other areas. Thankfully the Bible promises that God will always forgive your sin, too. In fact, the Bible states God will *faithfully* forgive your sins (1 John 1:9).

No matter how much you mess up or get spiritually dirty, God will forgive and still use you to do great things. Remember that God will forgive all sins. Seek forgiveness and make a plan of action to stay *clean* the next time!

Application Questions:

» What kinds of sinful choices <u>seem</u> to make someone more spiritually *dirty* than others?

» Is it even possible for one type of sin to be *dirtier* than another sin?

» Are you stuck in a sin that is messing you up and making you spiritually *unclean*?

» If you are stuck in a sin, what expert in your life can help you make positive and God-pleasing choices?

Book's Main Takeaway

Life can be hard! Life can be uncomfortably frustrating. Who knew that monster trucks could teach us so much about life, though?

Next time you watch monster trucks do tricks, races, and jumps, remember there is a lot that goes on behind the scenes. Please do not give up when life gets too *bumpy*. There is a bigger picture to consider. God is up to something good. I encourage you to remember God's promises of strength and comfort.

Remember what Ms. Emily taught: it is good to <u>believe in God</u>. Life is much more bearable, though, if you do more than just believe <u>in</u> Him. You must also <u>believe God</u> and His promises.

How to Become a Child of God

If you are unsure that you are a child of God (some call it being "saved" or "being a Christian"), here is how to become a child of God. Let's look at the "ABCs" of salvation.

A: <u>ADMIT</u> YOU ARE A SINNER.

> For all have sinned and fall short of the glory of God. (Romans 3:23)

A sin is anything you do that goes against what the Bible teaches. Examples include lying, disobeying, unkindness, not doing your best, etc. Everyone is guilty of sin. This sin separates humans from God.

B: <u>BELIEVE</u> THAT JESUS CHRIST DIED FOR YOUR SIN.
(He rose from the dead, too, because He is God.)

> But God demonstrates His own love toward us, in that while we were still sinners, Christ died for us. (Romans 5:8)

> And the angel said to the women, "Do not be afraid; for I know that you are looking for Jesus who has been crucified. He is not here, for He has risen, just as He said..." (Matthew 28:5-6a)

He died on a cross as the payment for your sin. Without Jesus' sacrifice, you would be stuck in your sin with no hope for forgiveness.

C: <u>CALL</u> TO GOD (IN PRAYER) TO SAVE YOU FROM YOUR SIN.

For everyone who calls on the name of the LORD will be saved (Romans 10:13).

There is nothing you can do to earn salvation. The Bible teaches salvation is by faith and not through any good works (Ephesians 2:8-9).

Here is a refreshing thing! You do not have to worry if you are good enough for God. God just wants you to have faith in Him. He is the way to salvation.

Here is an example of prayer to become a child of God:

> God, I know I am a sinner and do bad things. I believe that Jesus died as the payment for my sin. I accept this as the only way I can be saved. Please come into my life and save me.
>
> Amen

WITH YOUR FAITH PLACED IN JESUS, YOU ARE THEN A CHILD OF GOD.

Acknowledgments

I had a blast writing this book! To my two children, thank you for encouraging me to write a children's book on this topic. I love your desire to learn.

Thank you to my husband who gave me the time to write another book. As always, your technological help is especially appreciated!

Here is a special thank you to the experts who shared unique and fun monster truck facts with me. Brianna Mahon, I feel blessed to have communicated with you. I learned much from you and am now one of your biggest Monster Jam ® fans! Thank you to the Monster Jam ® Crew Chief who willingly answered several technical questions.

The Monster Jam ® world is an amazing place!

Thank you to my neighbor, Michael Novotny. Since you build vehicles, you were helpful in double-checking that I worded the mechanical parts appropriately.

Mrs. Lisa Lawrence, I genuinely appreciate your assistance to get this book cleaned up and ready to go as the process was starting.

To professional sports photographer, Andrew Fielder, I am grateful for your professionalism and help to secure your monster truck photographs.

Most of all, thank you to God for opening doors for this book to become a reality. His grace, even through the *bumps*, is one of my greatest blessings.

Bibliography

Books:

Buffy Silverman, *How Do Monster Trucks Work?* (Minneapolis: Lerner Publications, 2016).

Ian Graham, *MEGA MACHINES MONSTER TRUCKS* (Minneapolis: Lerner Publisher Services, 2016).

John Farndon, *Stickmen's Guide to Trains and Automobiles* (Minneapolis: Lerner Publications, 2016).

John MacArthur, *The MacArthur Bible Commentary* (Nashville: Thomas Nelson, 2005).

Kiel Phegley, *Monster Jam Official Guidebook, Monster-Sized* (New York: Scholastic Inc., 2017).

Matt Doeden, *MONSTER TRUCKS* (North Mankato, Minnesota: Capstone Press, 2019).

Quinn M. Arnold, *Monster Trucks* (Mankato, Minnesota: Creative Education, Creative Paperbacks, 2017).

Tedd Arnold, *Fly Guy Presents: Monster Trucks* (New York: Scholastic Inc., 2019).

Interviews:

Brad Williams, interview by author, April 17, 2021.
Brianna Mahon, interview by author, December 20, 2021.
Crew Chief, unnamed at his request, interview by author, December 21, 2021.
Emily Woodlee, personal message, December 26, 2021.
Mike Novotny, interview by author, January 22, 2022.

Websites:

https://cdn.monsterjam.com/2020-05/MJ-Monster-Shocks-Education-Packet-02_0.pdf , accessed December 17, 2021.

https://cdn.monsterjam.com/2020-05/MJTA-Ceda-Fair-Education-Packet-01.pdf, accessed December 27, 2021.

https://cdn.monsterjam.com/2020-05/MJTA-Cedar-Fair-Education-Packet-02.pdf, accessed December 23, 2021.

https://www.monsterjam.com/en-US/monster-jam-101, accessed December 19, 2021.

https://www.monsterjam.com/en-US/videos/winning-high-jump-cynthia-gauthier-world-finals-xx, accessed January 14, 2022.

https://www.monsterjam.com/en-US/news/saturday-action-monster-jam-world-finals-xx,accessed April 16, 2022.

Monster Jam, "Monster Jam – 2020 – Angel Stadium – Anaheim CA – 2," November 24, 2020, video, 26:30, https://www.youtube.com/watch?v=8llRKMFS3nM, accessed July 10, 2021.

CPSIA information can be obtained
at www.ICGtesting.com
Printed in the USA
BVHW062203021022
648493BV00007B/119